COVER
TO
COVER

To all the wonderful staff at Gomer who have been so supportive
and a great encouragement over many years

First published in 2012 by Pont Books, an imprint of
Gomer Press, Llandysul, Ceredigion, SA44 4JL
www.gomer.co.uk

The publishers would like to thank Adrian Willford for permission
to reproduce the photograph on page 31.

ISBN 978 1 84851 467 6

A CIP record for this title is available from the British Library.

This book is published with the financial support of the
Welsh Books Council.

Printed and bound in Wales at Gomer Press, Llandysul, Ceredigion

COVER TO COVER

How a book is made

ROB LEWIS

Pont

A book starts with a story. The person who writes the story is called an AUTHOR. A story starts with an idea . . .

Sometimes it is very hard to think of an idea.

When the author gets a good idea he writes it down. Some authors write on paper but most use a computer.

It can take a long time to find the right words.

Sometimes research is needed.

At last the story is finished.
The author prints it out.
This is called the TYPESCRIPT.

Some books have pictures, like this one. The pictures are drawn by the ILLUSTRATOR. In this book the author is also the illustrator.

The author/illustrator divides the text up into paragraphs so there are words on each page of the book. He sometimes draws thumbnail sketches as he thinks of new ideas.

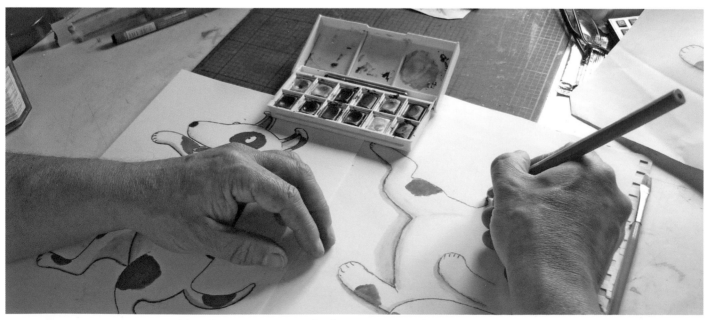

He does some rough drawings of the main characters in the story.

Then he makes small drawings for each page in the book and writes or types in the words where he thinks they ought to go on the page.

Each picture is stuck onto a big sheet of paper so that you can see the whole story like a cartoon strip. This is called a STORYBOARD.

The author/illustrator sends the typescript and the storyboard to the PUBLISHING HOUSE. The publisher who made this book is called GOMER PRESS.

The typescript and storyboard arrive on the desk of an EDITOR. Gomer Press gets lots of stories from other authors and illustrators. The editors read through them and choose the best ones to publish.

This will be a great story for Gomer.

Here are Sioned and Viv, the Welsh and English children's editors. They decide how many copies to print, the size of the book, the type of paper (matt or shiny), and the number of pages.

We'll print 5,000 copies. It's a 32-page picture book which will measure 215 mm x 270 mm.

The author then receives a CONTRACT. A contract is a promise. The publisher promises to pay the author a ROYALTY. The author promises to help with any changes and to finish all the work on time.

The editor suggests slight changes to the story to make it better.

The editor talks to the DESIGNER about the cover. The designer suggests ideas for the cover image and design. He chooses the TYPEFACE and decides where to put the title, the author's name, the blurb, the price and the publishing details.

Sometimes the illustrator designs the cover illustration.

The designer will also choose the book's layout, where the words and pictures will go. He and the editor will decide on the FONT for the inside pages, and also the POINT size.

This is called Arial. The size is 12 point or 12 pt.

This is called Times New Roman and the size is 14 pt.

This font is New Century Schoolbook and the size is 20 pt.

This font is called Lucida Sans and is in 26 pt.

Next the editor tells the illustrator he can start painting the pictures. She may send layouts with text in place so the illustrator knows how big to make the pictures and where to put them on the page.

The illustrator uses his storyboard as a guide when painting the illustrations. He sketches them out in pencil first. If the storyboard images are good enough, sometimes he enlarges them on the computer and traces them onto his drawing board.

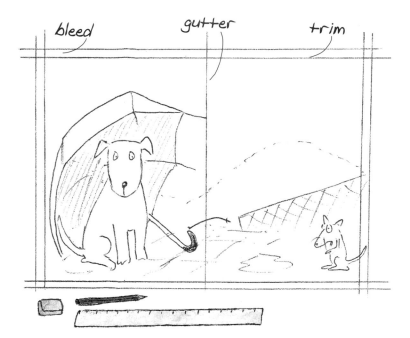

He must be careful not to put important details in the GUTTER or at the edges. He paints an extra bit, called a BLEED, so that there won't be any white edges showing when the pages are trimmed.

Illustrators can use pastels, chalks, inks, watercolours, acrylic paints or coloured pencils to do the pictures. This illustrator uses all of them!

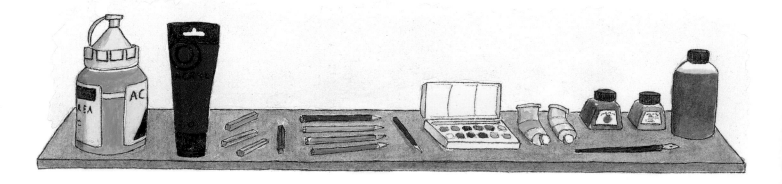

As the illustrator paints, he adds extra details. There are 29 pages to complete, as well as the cover illustration. The artwork can take a long time. This illustrator takes about two months to do a book.

At last it is finished. The illustrator wraps the parcel of pictures very carefully and posts it to the publisher.

When the artwork arrives, the editor checks for any mistakes. The illustrator might have to alter a picture or even a whole page. Sometimes it can be altered on the computer.

Then all the pictures are scanned onto the computer. Some publishers use a drum scanner. The artwork is wrapped around a drum and it is scanned as the drum revolves. This book was scanned using a FLATBED SCANNER.

The cover goes to the MARKETING department. They can use the image to create posters and other publicity materials to promote the book before it is published.

The scanned pictures are added to the text in a special computer program. Then copies called PROOFS of each page are printed out. There may still be mistakes to correct in the layout, words, punctuation and spelling. Another editor, Rhian, is helping Viv and Sioned with the checking.

Proofs are sent to the author for another check.

Finally the book is ready to send to print. A computer program arranges the pages so that they will be in the correct position on the printing plates. There will be 8 pages on each plate. The order looks odd at this stage.

8	1
9	16
12	13
5	4

6	3
11	14
10	15
7	2

24	17
25	32
28	29
21	20

22	19
27	30
26	31
23	18

Some books printed only in black and white are produced on new machines, like giant photocopiers, that do not need printing plates. In the future, colour books may be printed in this way too. This book was produced on a traditional printing press.

Printing plates are made in a special plate-imaging machine. Lasers transfer the text and pictures onto metal sheets and chemical washes develop the plates ready for the press. The platemaker checks that the pages are in the right order on the plates.

There will be one plate for each colour, and there are 4 colours altogether.

Cyan

Magenta

Yellow

Black

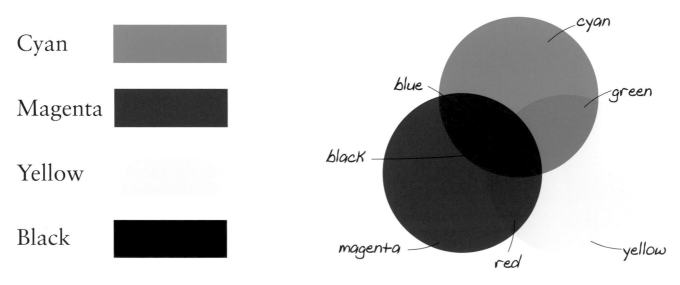

When these colours are mixed (by printing on top of each other) they produce all the colours needed for a full-colour picture book. A novel in black and white will only need one plate.

For a 32-page picture book there will be 4 plates × 4 colours, which makes a total of 16 plates. The cover is printed separately on special card.

The plates are taken to the press and placed on the printing drums.

This is the giant 4-colour printing press. The sheets of paper are fed through the press from right to left. The ink goes onto the printing plate through a set of rollers.

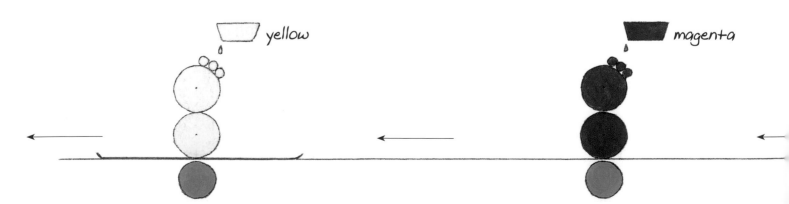

yellow

magenta

The press is running smoothly.

The ink is transferred from the printing plate onto a blanket and then onto the paper. The colours are printed one after the other. The temperature is kept hot inside the press so that the inks dry quickly.

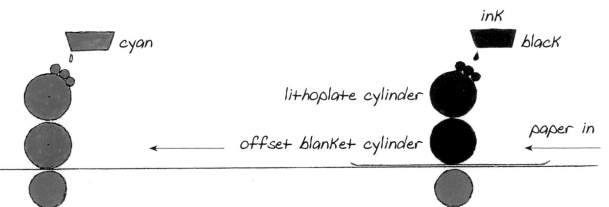

cyan

ink

black

lithoplate cylinder

offset blanket cylinder

paper in

The printed sheets are then fed flat into the folding machine. The paper is folded automatically and comes out as a 16-page section with the pages in the correct order. Two sections are needed to make a picture book. More sections are needed to make a novel or a longer story book.

edges not trimmed yet

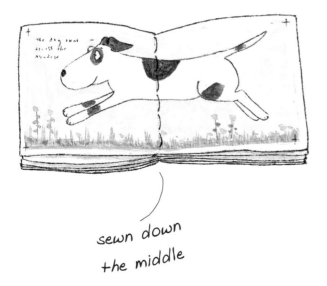

sewn down
the middle

In some books, like novels, the sections are glued together. Picture books are usually sewn to make them stronger.

A special gathering machine will pick up the separate sections of the book and put them together in the right order and the right way up.

Hopefully there are no sections upside down or in the wrong order, though this sometimes does happen!

The covers are laminated in the laminating machine to protect them and give them a nice finish.

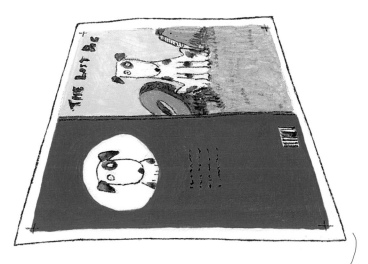

A shiny plastic coating is melted on. Some covers are very shiny. Others have a smooth matt finish.

The book's covers are glued to the inside sections in the bookbinding machine.

The spine is creased so the pages turn better.

glue

Then the book is trimmed in the three-knife trimmer, which cuts three sides all at once.

The edges are all trimmed – there are lots of bits left over to be recycled.

At last the book is finished! The author gets free copies to give to family and friends.

The marketing department gets free copies to send to book reviewers so that they can write about the book in their magazines and newspapers. Good reviews will help the book sell more copies.

The book is entered for prizes and awards. If the book wins a prize it will also help to sell more copies.

The book will appear in the publisher's catalogue. Sales representatives will visit schools, libraries and bookshops, encouraging the staff to order copies of the book.

The rights department will try to sell the book to other countries. The book will then be printed in other languages, as well as Welsh and English. Can you guess which languages these books are in?

The books are put into boxes and stored in a huge warehouse. Deep shelves stretch from floor to ceiling and a forklift truck is needed to reach the boxes on the highest shelves. Each title is carefully numbered and recorded on the computer. The warehouse manager needs to know where all the books are stored so that he can find them when required.

Smaller numbers of each title are kept on the PICKING SHELVES which you can see on the left of the photograph. People contact Aled by email or phone with their book orders. He collects the books from the picking shelves and arranges for the order to be sent out.

Then lorries and vans pick up the books and deliver them to schools . . .

libraries . . .

bookshops, and maybe . . .

. . . to your house!

Though you can read books on computers, phones and other electronic devices, there will always be a place for books made from paper. I hope you have enjoyed this one!

A word from the author . . . and the illustrator!

I'm Rob Lewis, the author and the illustrator of *Cover to Cover*,
and this is a photograph of me winning the Tir Na n-Og award with my book
Three Little Sheep. I've written and illustrated more than 40 books, not to mention
the ones where I illustrated somebody else's story.

I'm often asked what it's like to be famous and the answer is that I don't really
know. After working with some of the big London publishing companies, I now
live in a sleepy part of mid Wales where I enjoy gardening and working at various
book projects. What I like best, though, is getting out to schools and libraries to
meet and work with children. If I can inspire someone else to read, tell their own
story, write it down or draw the pictures, I feel my visit has been worthwhile.

I first worked with Pont Books back in 2002 when we published *Cold Jac*
together. Pont is part of Gomer Press, a printing and publishing company based in
Llandysul, west Wales. Gomer has been in existence since 1892 and celebrated
its 120th birthday in 2012. Although it is the biggest publishing company in Wales,
it is still a family business: the current managing director, Jonathan Lewis, is the
great-grandson of the company's founder. On the final page of the book you will
see a photograph of Jonathan with his father and his brother.

Gomer Press has always published books in English and in Welsh. It makes me
very proud that my books appear in both languages.

Diolch yn fawr, Gwasg Gomer!

Jonathan Lewis, Rod Lewis and John H. Lewis with an old-fashioned printing press.